What Makes Me A
HINDU?

Charles George

**KIDHAVEN
PRESS**™

THOMSON

GALE

San Diego • Detroit • New York • San Francisco • Cleveland
New Haven, Conn. • Waterville, Maine • London • Munich

THOMSON

✳ ™

GALE

© 2004 by KidHaven Press. KidHaven Press is an imprint of Thomson Gale, a part of the Thomson Corporation. Thomson is a trademark and Gale are registered trademarks used herein under license.

KidHaven™ and Thomson Learning™ are trademarks used herein under license.

For more information, contact
KidHaven Press
27500 Drake Rd.
Farmington Hills, MI 48331-3535
Or you can visit our Internet site at http://www.gale.com

LIBRARY OF CONGRESS CATALOGING-IN-PUBLICATION DATA

George, Charles, 1949–
  Hindu / by Charles George.
    p. cm. — (What Makes Me A?))
Includes bibliographical references (p.   ).
Summary: Discusses Hinduism including how Hinduism began, what Hindus believe, how they practice their faith, and what holidays they celebrate.
  ISBN 0-7377-2267-3
  1. Hinduism—Juvenile literature. [1. Hinduism.] I. Title. II. Series.
  BL1203.G5 2004
  294.5—dc22
                                  2003024346

CONTENTS

INTRODUCTION

A Common Heritage

Hinduism is one of the world's oldest religions. Its origin traces back thousands of years. It is the world's third largest religion. Only Christianity and Islam have more followers. Worldwide, more than 828 million people are Hindus. Most Hindus, almost 822 million, live in southern Asia—in India, Nepal, Malaysia, and Sri Lanka.

Hindu is a Persian word for "Indian." Muslim invaders first used the term about A.D. 1200 to describe the religion practiced there. Most Hindus call their beliefs *sanatana dharma,* "eternal law" or "eternal teaching."

Hinduism is unique among the world's religions. It is a combination of ancient religions whose origins are unknown. Also unknown is the identity of the founder, or founders, of Hinduism. Finally, Hindus consider more than one text sacred. Their holy books include the Vedas, the Upanishads, and two epic poems, the *Ramayana* and the *Mahabharata.*

Hindus bathe in the Ganges River in India to help them achieve salvation. More than 828 million people around the world are Hindus.

Unlike other religions, Hinduism is loosely organized. There are Hindu priests, but no priest is ranked higher than another. Also, Hindus may worship in a variety of ways. No method is considered better than another. However they choose to worship, all Hindus share a common heritage that goes back centuries.

CHAPTER ONE

How Did My Religion Begin?

Because Hinduism is such an ancient religion, dating back forty-five hundred years, it has been shaped by many different religions and cultures. The religion has changed a great deal over the centuries due to new ideas, new teachers, or new interpretations of holy texts.

Indus Valley Civilization

Between 2500 and 1750 B.C. a civilization flourished in the Indus River Valley in what is now Pakistan. Its major cities were Harappa and Mohenjo Daro. Knowledge of this early Indus Valley civilization is limited because its written language has not been translated.

However, archaeological findings, particularly clay figurines and tablets, suggest that elements of the Indus religion helped form the basis of early Hinduism and are still part of modern Hinduism. Apparently, the

Indus religion was based on nature worship, with many gods and goddesses. Bulls and other animals were probably worshipped. Hindus still worship many gods and consider cows sacred.

Another element of Indus worship that has passed down to modern Hinduism is the belief that water, especially water flowing in a river, is holy. The Indus River was holy to this ancient civilization, and today's Hindus consider the Ganges River sacred.

Finally, the Indus religion may have included yoga, a system of exercise and meditation designed to bring peace of mind and physical fitness. Hindus today still practice yoga.

The Indus River flows down from the Himalayas through Pakistan. Archaeological discoveries in this area suggest that early Hinduism began here.

Aryan Invasion

Between 1500 and 1200 B.C. a group known as
Aryans, or Noble Ones, invaded the Indus River Valley. Scientists do not know exactly where the Aryans
came from. Some say their homeland was in what is
now southern Russia. Others believe they migrated
from eastern Europe. Soon after they arrived in India,
they ruled the region. Their religion mixed with that of
the Indus Valley to form the beginnings of Hinduism.

Scientists know more about Aryan religion because
the Aryan written language, Sanskrit, has been translated. Aryan religion, according to the written records,
was rich in mythology—stories of their many gods and
goddesses that helped explain elements of nature.
Aryans worshipped thirty-three main gods and goddesses that represented forces of nature—sun, moon,
sky, sea, storms, and wind. Chief among them was
Indra, god of the atmosphere, storms, and war. Below
him were Mitra and Varuna, gods of the sun, and Agni,
god of sacrificial fire. Animal sacrifice was part of their
religion.

According to their writings, Aryans were originally
nomads, moving from place to place. Their lives cen-
tered on tending and grazing herds of livestock from
which they got milk and butter. During religious ceremonies they threw offerings of butter, grain, and spice
into a ceremonial fire while chanting sacred hymns.
These hymns are known as *Vedas*, a Sanskrit word
which means "wisdom" or "knowledge." Milk and butter are important elements of modern Hindu worship,

still used as gifts to the gods, but modern Hindus rarely practice animal sacrifice.

Aryan worship in the home began with simple ceremonies. Stories of gods and how to worship them were passed from generation to generation within each family. As their civilization became more complex, religious ceremonies also became more complex, requiring specially trained priests to conduct them. Aryans believed ritual and sacrifice had to be performed correctly to please the gods, so the status of priests rose.

Eventually, Aryan society became organized into strict social classes called castes. At the top were priests, followed by rulers, warriors, artisans, merchants, then unskilled workers, farmers, and peasants. Because they could read, the priests' position at the top of Aryan society became even more secure when the Vedas were written down between 1500 and 1000 B.C. The Vedas became Hinduism's first sacred books.

Aryans worshipped thirty-three gods and goddesses, including Indra (pictured), the god of the atmosphere, storms, and war.

The Vedas and Upanishads

The Vedas are the world's oldest religious books, and Hindus believe they came directly from Brahman, their main god. Three powerful gods in Hinduism, each a part of Brahman, are first mentioned in the Vedas—Brahma, the Creator; Vishnu, the Protector; and Shiva, the Destroyer.

The oldest and most important Veda is the Rigveda, or Songs of Knowledge. This work contains the story of creation, 1,028 hymns to Aryan gods, and explains why there are social classes. Along with three other Vedas, it formed the basis of early Hindu religious practice, as did the Bible for Christianity, the Torah for Judaism, and the Koran for Islam.

Several centuries later, between 800 and 300 B.C., priests whose identities are unknown wrote other texts to help explain the Vedas. Among these are the Upanishads, which means "lessons" or "sitting at the feet of the master." This work introduces the idea that Brah-

Priests were at the top of Aryan society because they could read.

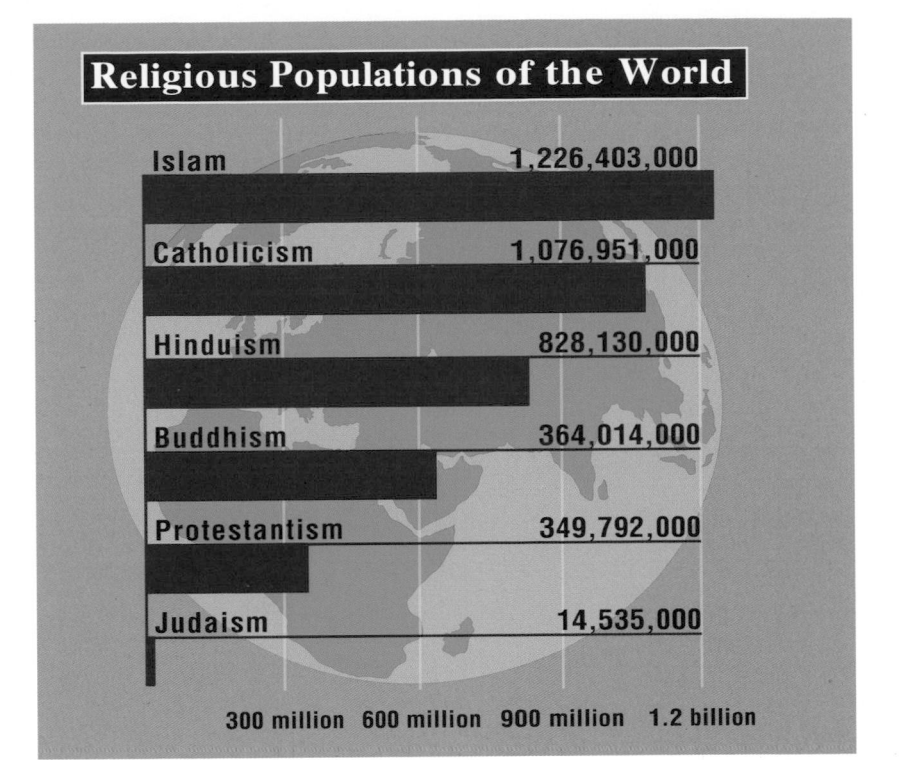

Religious Populations of the World

Religion	Population
Islam	1,226,403,000
Catholicism	1,076,951,000
Hinduism	828,130,000
Buddhism	364,014,000
Protestantism	349,792,000
Judaism	14,535,000

300 million 600 million 900 million 1.2 billion

man is pure spirit and the one supreme being in the universe. All village, nature, family, and personal gods are simply different aspects of him. The Upanishads also teach that Brahman's universal soul is in everything, especially in each person's soul, or atman. This idea is similar to the Holy Spirit of the Christian faith.

New Religions and Hindu Epics

In the centuries following the Upanishads, events took place that further changed the way Hindus thought of the universe and their place in it. Around 500 B.C. two new religions broke away from traditional Hinduism. Buddhism and Jainism share many of Hinduism's beliefs, but their founders, Siddhartha Gautama (known as the Buddha) and Vardhamana (known as Mahavira, or Great Hero) focused on making life better on Earth instead of on worshipping the gods.

Between 400 B.C. and A.D. 400, unidentified poets composed two epic poems—the *Ramayana* and the *Mahabharata*—that increased Hinduism's popular appeal in India. Each contains tales from Hindu mythology—stories of gods and goddesses, epic battles against evil, and heroic deeds similar to those found in Greek and Roman mythology. Along with the new philosophies of Buddhism and Jainism, these epics, with themes of personal sacrifice, honor, duty, and love of God, helped Hinduism move from a religion of strict ritual to one of personal devotion.

The Bhagavad Gita

The text that most helped create this sense of personal devotion is a relatively short section of the *Mahabharata* called the Bhagavad Gita, or "Song of the Lord." This is the most popular sacred text of Hinduism and has become the heart of modern Hindu philosophy.

In the Gita a young prince, Arjuna, is about to go into battle against members of his own royal family. He hesitates, worried that he is not doing the right thing. His chariot driver, Krishna, explains to Arjuna what his duties are and that the soul is immortal and cannot be killed. He also tells Arjuna that knowledge, work, and devotion are paths to salvation, which is open to everyone.

Krishna, like Rama, the hero of the *Ramayana*, turns out to be the god Vishnu in human form. During his dis-

In this scene from the *Mahabharata,* Krishna and Arjuna leave for battle. The tales of the *Mahabharata* helped increase Hinduism's popularity in India

cussion with Arjuna, he answers some of the most important questions a person can ask: Why are we here? How should we live? What is God? Because of its positive and loving message, the Gita has inspired not only Hindus but people of all faiths around the world.

CHAPTER TWO

What Do I Believe?

Hinduism today is a complex mixture of ancient Indus nature worship, Aryan ritual, and personal devotion to God. In fact, there are as many ways to worship as a Hindu as there are Hindus. However they worship, all Hindus share certain common beliefs.

Brahman and the Atman

According to Hindu philosophy, the universe has always existed and will always exist in a constant state of change—the "Days and Nights of Brahman." Just as a person breathes in and out, the universe goes through an unending cycle of existence called "the breath of God." This cycle, according to Hindu texts, lasts 4.5 billion years.

All Hindus believe in the existence of Brahman. He is the World Soul, the collective soul, without beginning or end. He is the supreme being, the creator of life and the life force that powers the universe. To Hindus, he is all around—in every rock, tree, and stream. He exists in every living creature.

Since every living creature is part of Brahman, God is in all living beings. For that reason, all life is sacred. Hindus believe everyone should practice ahimsa—nonviolence or noninjury—and refuse to cause harm to any living being. This belief leads most Hindus to be vegetarian.

Hindus believe that all life is sacred, so most Hindus are vegetarian.

They refuse to eat meat because a living creature was killed to provide it. Others refuse to wear leather or fur for the same reason. Some believe so strongly in this concept that they wear cloth masks over their mouths to avoid accidentally swallowing small insects.

Hindus today seldom worship Brahman directly. Instead, they worship three gods considered part of him—Brahma, Vishnu, and Shiva. Each performs a different function in the cycle of life.

Brahma

Brahma, a god of knowledge, creates the universe. He is pictured with four heads, often bearded, facing in four directions. He has four hands, in which he carries the Vedas and at times a water pot (signifying prosperity), a spoon, a string of pearls, a staff, or a bowl. He can be depicted with red or pink skin and wearing a white robe and a sacred cord across the shoulder.

Vishnu

Vishnu is the preserver of the world and the keeper of morality and order. At various times during the existence of the universe, Vishnu takes on human form and lives on Earth to guide all living beings. According to Hindus, there have been many incarnations of Vishnu. Some believe the latest were Buddha, Jesus, and Muhammad. Most followers of Vishnu worship his two most popular incarnations, Rama and Krishna.

Vishnu, like Brahma, is sometimes pictured with four heads and four arms and hands. He can be depicted holding a conch shell, a prayer wheel, a discus, and a

Brahma (left) is the god of knowledge and creator of the universe. He is often pictured with four heads and four hands.

The Hindu god Vishnu is the preserver of the world. Seen here as Rama, he is believed to sleep for four months of the year on a sea serpent.

lotus. He has a hairy chest and wears a sacred stone around his neck. In some temples, though, his image is only a pair of bare feet. Some Hindus believe his magnificence is beyond human comprehension. He is believed to sleep for four months each year, resting on a sea serpent with a lotus sprouting from his navel.

Shiva

Shiva is considered both a creator and a destroyer. At some point in the life of the universe Shiva dissolves it, and time enters the "Night of Brahman." This act of destruction is what Hindus believe leads again and again to the re-creation of the universe.

In images portraying Shiva as the Lord of the Dance, Shiva is dancing. He represents the energy that flows through the world causing day and night, the seasons, and birth and death. He usually has four arms and holds a bow, a club, a drum, and a noose. As he dances he tramples under his feet the dwarf of ignorance.

Reincarnation and Karma

Hindus believe every person has an eternal soul, or atman. They believe atman is part of Brahman. We are spirits who live inside our bodies, the same as people wear clothes or live in houses. When we change clothes, or move to a different house, we are still the same.

Since the soul of each living creature is part of Brahman, it is immortal. It cannot die. However, it has to keep coming back to Earth to learn the lessons of life until it perfects itself. At that point, a time Hindus call *moksha,* or "salvation," the atman goes to join Brahman as pure spirit and does not have to return to Earth. This is the ultimate goal of every Hindu.

Hindus believe each soul goes through eighty-four thousand incarnations on Earth—an almost endless cycle of birth, death, and rebirth. Each soul begins as the lowest life-form—a germ or virus, for example—and progresses automatically from one life-form to another until it is reborn as a human being. Once human, the rules change. Humans become self-aware and can choose how they behave.

This is where karma comes in. Karma is the law of cause and effect. Whatever people do or do not do affects their futures. Every thought that people have affects their futures. Good thoughts and deeds bring good. Bad thoughts and deeds bring misfortune. This explains why some people seem to have easy lives, while others face one hardship after another. It also explains why some people are born with talents and abilities others do not have. People with more talents and easier lives are farther along the path to salvation. Thus, every life is a lesson to be learned or an opportunity missed.

For Hindus, then, how a person lives life on Earth is extremely important. A person who does bad things and thinks bad thoughts remains ignorant of the true nature of

Worshippers offer gifts to Shiva in Calcutta, India. Shiva is revered as both a creator and destroyer.

humanity and goes through many painful lifetimes. To Hindus, people make their own heaven and hell on Earth with their attitudes, thoughts, and deeds.

Different Paths

Hindus believe everyone will eventually achieve salvation and unite with Brahman. They also believe that, since people have different personalities and different talents, they approach problems in different ways. So for Hindus there are four general paths, or yogas, to follow to achieve *moksha*. These are the path of knowledge, the path of love, the path of work, and the path of meditation and physical discipline. People are encouraged to try each one or to combine aspects of several to find what suits them best. Within each yoga, of course, there are an infinite number of ways to proceed.

Besides different pathways to salvation, Hindus recognize that other religions may also achieve the same goal. Hindus are open to the beliefs and practices of other faiths. When someone asked Mohandas Gandhi, the leader of India's independence from the British Empire, if he were Hindu, he replied that he was Hindu, Christian, Muslim, Jew, and Buddhist. He believed in the essential truth of all of the world's religions.

CHAPTER THREE

How Do I Practice My Faith?

To Hindus, worship is a private matter. Hindus usually worship individually rather than with a group. Most Hindu worship, or *puja*, takes place at specially built shrines in the home, but shrines are also found along city streets, in temples, and at locations considered holy. Unlike most religions, there are no set rules for worship. Hindus worship in their own ways, whenever and wherever they choose.

Priests may assist with worship, and some Hindu families have their own family priest who comes to their home to conduct ceremonies. Priests are members of the Brahmin caste and are trained from childhood to conduct rituals and to memorize the holy texts.

For Hindus, every action and thought has religious meaning. In the Bhagavad Gita, for example, Krishna tells Arjuna that the way to salvation is to make all of life an act of worship. This is what devout Hindus strive for.

Puja, Acts of Devotion

Home Shrines

Domestic shrines may be elaborate rooms with sculptures of the favorite gods, one corner devoted to worship, or a simple shelf with pictures of the gods. Every shrine has two elements—fire and water—used for purification. Some have a mandala (a drawing representing the universe) along with incense, flowers, food offerings, and colored powder for decoration.

The daily *puja* takes place three times each day—early in the morning, at noon, and in the evening. It usually begins with ceremonial bathing of the worshipper and the god. Chanting, repeating the god's name, reciting

Hindus usually worship alone and whenever they choose at shrines in the home, along the street, or in temples.

prayers from scriptures, and applying perfume to the image are common practices. Worshippers offer food and flowers to the god, symbolic gifts to show their gratitude. They might place single blooms or garlands of lotus, marigold, rose, or jasmine, as well as milk, fruit, honey, rice, sweet breads, or sandalwood paste before images of their gods. They burn incense in the shrine to symbolically carry their prayers to the gods.

Temples

Most Hindu temples, or *mandir,* are devoted to the worship of one Hindu god. Some, however, are dedicated to a particular sadhu, or holy man. Each temple has its own priest who performs the *puja* ceremony and cares for the image of the god. Priests also help people read and study the holy books and learn about their religion. Some temples in India's larger cities are ornate and large enough to hold hundreds of individual worshippers. In rural villages, poverty usually dictates a smaller shrine, either in a simple building or under a canopy in the open air.

A typical city temple is an enclosed area with several open-air shrines. It is a place for prayer, meditation, and celebration. It can also be noisy and lively, filled with the sounds of individuals worshipping in their own way— praying aloud, chanting, or singing. The main shrine room is generally in a building topped with a pointed tower, or *shikara.* Access to this area is limited to priests. Other worshippers observe from outside, bowing, praying to the image, and offering small gifts.

Hindu temples are usually devoted to the worship of one god. The Lakshmana Temple in Khajuraho, India, is dedicated to Vishnu.

Also on the grounds are containers of *tulasi,* a basil plant whose leaves are used in religious ceremonies, and a ceremonial chariot, or *rath,* used to transport the god's image during parades. A memorial shrine where bodies of local saints are buried and secondary shrines honoring other gods complete the temple grounds.

Worship in a temple is similar to that performed in domestic shrines. Male worshippers remove their shoes and female worshippers cover their heads as signs of respect before entering the temple. Worshippers wash their feet, hands, and faces, and rinse their mouths. They might sing hymns, ring bells, burn incense, play music, or make offerings of food, flowers, or money. A priest sometimes reads passages from the Vedas.

Pilgrimages

Every year millions of Hindus set off on special journeys, called pilgrimages, to holy places. These can be temples, mountains, rivers, or locations mentioned in sacred texts. They go to pray for something special, to offer thanks to a particular god, or because they feel the journey helps them move closer to salvation.

The seven holiest cities in India are called *tirthas,* or "crossing places." Most of them are on the banks of major rivers. They are Varanasi, Ajodhya, Mathura, Haridwar, Ujjain, Dwarka, and Kanchipuram. The first four are on the banks of the Ganges, considered India's most sacred river. The holiest of these is Varanasi.

The ancient city of Varanasi contains hundreds of temples. Most are dedicated to Shiva, because legends say Shiva chose Varanasi as his home on Earth. For four miles along the banks of the Ganges, seventy sets of stone steps, or ghats, lead to the river. They serve as platforms for cremations and as entrances to the purifying waters of the Ganges.

Water from the Ganges is holy, and pilgrims believe bathing in it and drinking it helps achieve salvation. They also take it home for use in household and temple rituals.

The Cradle of Hinduism

PAKISTAN

Indus River

Himalayas

NEPAL

Haridwar

New Delhi

Mathura

Ganges River

Ajodhya

INDIA

Varanasi

Ujjain

Dwarka is the legendary kingdom of Krishna (pictured).

Dwarka

Arabian Sea

Bay of Bengal

Kanchipuram

Varanasi, considered the holiest city of India, sits on the banks of the Ganges River.

The town of Kanchipuram is dedicated to Shiva (pictured) and Vishnu.

Thousands come to Varanasi to die, and thousands more come to cremate relatives or sprinkle their ashes into the Ganges. For Indians who cannot make the pilgrimage to the Ganges, any water, even tap water, can be used for these purification rituals. Water, though, is but one of Hinduism's religious symbols.

Religious Symbols

In all religions symbols are important. This is especially true of Hinduism. Certain objects, images, and sounds are special for Hindus, especially images of gods. Paintings and sculptures of Vishnu, Shiva, and Brahma fill temples, streets, and homes.

Besides the three primary gods, images of other popular gods are widely displayed. Ganesha, the elephant-headed son of Shiva, is the god of wisdom and good luck. His image is often displayed above businesses and on the title pages of books. Hindus salute him for luck before going on a journey or before starting a business. Hanuman, the monkey-faced god, is an important character in the *Ramayana*. He is known for strength, speed, agility, courage, and loyalty. Athletes often ask him for help. Another popular image is Nandi, the white bull who carries Shiva. Followers honor him for strength and power.

"Om" is a sound Hindus consider sacred—a single syllable usually spoken at the beginning and at the end of Hindu chants. It is considered the original sound of creation—the sound that brought about creation and sustains the universe. Its written symbol, in Sanskrit, is seen throughout India.

The lotus is a symbol of Vishnu. It represents creation, rebirth, purity, and beauty. The swastika is an ancient Aryan symbol of peace. It is often drawn on cards and woven into cloth to bring good luck and to ward off bad luck.

Two Hindu religious symbols are sometimes difficult for Westerners to understand. For example, simple stone

Images of gods are important to Hindus, and they can be found in temples, in homes, and in the streets, like this statue of Shiva.

or marble carvings called lingams sometimes are used in temples to Shiva instead of Shiva's image. A lingam is a long, smooth stone representing Shiva's strength.

Another thing sacred to Hindus, perhaps the most widely known and the least understood, is the cow. In India, cows are allowed to wander the streets unbothered. They are sacred, partly because of Nandi, but also because cows give milk, and milk is considered one of the purest offerings to the gods. These symbols are present in the everyday lives of all Hindus, but are particularly important during special life events.

The lotus is a symbol of the god Vishnu, the keeper of morality and order.

Rites of Passage

Sixteen Hindu ceremonies mark particular stages in a person's life. These begin before a child is born and continue until death. Most are performed around the birth of the child.

Birth and Childhood

When a couple decides to have a child, they consult a priest to find out the best time of year to conceive to generate the best karma for the baby's new incarnation. During pregnancy, the mother recites prayers and makes offerings to ensure the baby's survival and good health. Parents often make offerings of rice to Vishnu to ask for his protection.

Ten or twelve days after the birth, a naming ceremony takes place. Again, a priest is consulted to determine the best combination of syllables for the child's name. He also explains the child's horoscope—the position of the stars and planets at the time of the child's birth—and how it will affect his or her life. After the ceremony, parents take the child on its first outing, often to a temple or shrine. When the baby first takes solid food, usually at five months, special prayers are offered.

By the time the child is five, its parents will have shaved its head in another ceremony. This symbolizes the removal of bad karma the child might have retained from a previous life.

Sacred Thread Ceremony

In some Hindu families, twelve-year-old boys undergo a ceremony to prepare them for marriage and to learn to lead their families in worship. The Sacred Thread, a loop of cotton thread made sacred by sprinkling it with water, is placed over the left shoulder and under the right arm. These cords are worn into adulthood.

Weddings

Hindu weddings are full of tradition and religious symbolism. In Indian culture it is common for parents to choose whom their children marry. Priests help decide which people are best suited to each other by comparing their horoscopes. They also help pick a lucky day for the wedding.

The ceremony, which can last several days, includes up to fifteen rituals. Most weddings involve prayers and songs of blessing, followed by the symbolic tying of the couple's wrists with a piece of cotton thread dyed with a yellow spice and sprinkled with water. The ceremony is not complete until the couple takes seven steps around the sacred fire, making a vow at each step and tossing grains of rice into the flames as an offering.

Death and Cremation

The final rite of passage takes place at death. If possible, just before a person dies relatives place three objects into the mouth of the dying person—a few drops of water from the sacred Ganges River, leaves of the sacred basil plant, *tulasi,* and a piece of gold. After death the body is bathed, wrapped in new cloth, and carried to a place to be cremated, or burned to ashes. If possible, Hindus perform this rite on the banks of a flowing river.

At the ceremony the eldest son drops tiny pieces of wood into the corpse's mouth, while others pile wood on

A Hindu bride and groom circle a ceremonial fire. Hindu weddings last several days and include many rituals.

the funeral pyre. As flames consume the body, relatives and priests recite prayers to help the soul journey to its next life. When the body burns, the skull cracks. Hindus believe this releases the soul for rebirth. After several hours, ashes and bones are scattered on the river.

Religious symbols and rituals form an important link between Hindus and their gods. They serve as constant reminders of the deeply personal relationship most Hindus feel toward their gods every day. They also play essential roles in Hindu holidays and festivals.

CHAPTER FOUR

What Holidays Do I Celebrate?

Although most Hindu worship is private and personal, Hindus celebrate hundreds of annual festivals or special celebrations. Some are huge celebrations, drawing millions of people. Others are small local celebrations, honoring a particular god, an event in a village's history, or a local sadhu.

National Festivals

All Hindus, regardless of which god they follow, where they live, or into which caste they were born, celebrate certain national Hindu festivals. The largest and most popular during the Hindu year are Holi, to welcome spring, Ganesha Chaturthi, to honor one of Hinduism's most popular gods, and Diwali, the Hindu Festival of Lights.

Holi

Holi, celebrated in March, is one of India's liveliest and messiest festivals. It celebrates the harvest of winter grain

Hindus dance in the streets of New Delhi, India, to celebrate Holi, a festival that welcomes spring.

and welcomes spring. It also honors Krishna. Bonfires, fireworks, dancing, and mischief are features of Holi. On the day of the festival, people wear their oldest clothes and throw brightly colored powder and water at each other. They do this in honor of stories of Krishna's youth, when he delighted in playing tricks on his companions. Later, revelers bathe, change clothes, and visit their relatives.

Ganesha Chaturthi

All Hindus love Ganesha, the elephant-headed god, because of his gentle nature. He is the remover of obstacles, the god of good luck, and almost every Hindu home has his image in their shrine. His is the most common image in

India. Most Hindus offer him a quick prayer before leaving the house, cooking a meal, or starting any project.

His annual celebration, called Ganesha Chaturthi, is a happy festival full of parades, music, singing, and laughter. At the beginning of the ten-day festival, families buy a brightly colored clay image of Ganesha. They carry it home, invite it into the house, and place it in a special

Images of the elephant-headed god Ganesha, the god of good luck, are common throughout India.

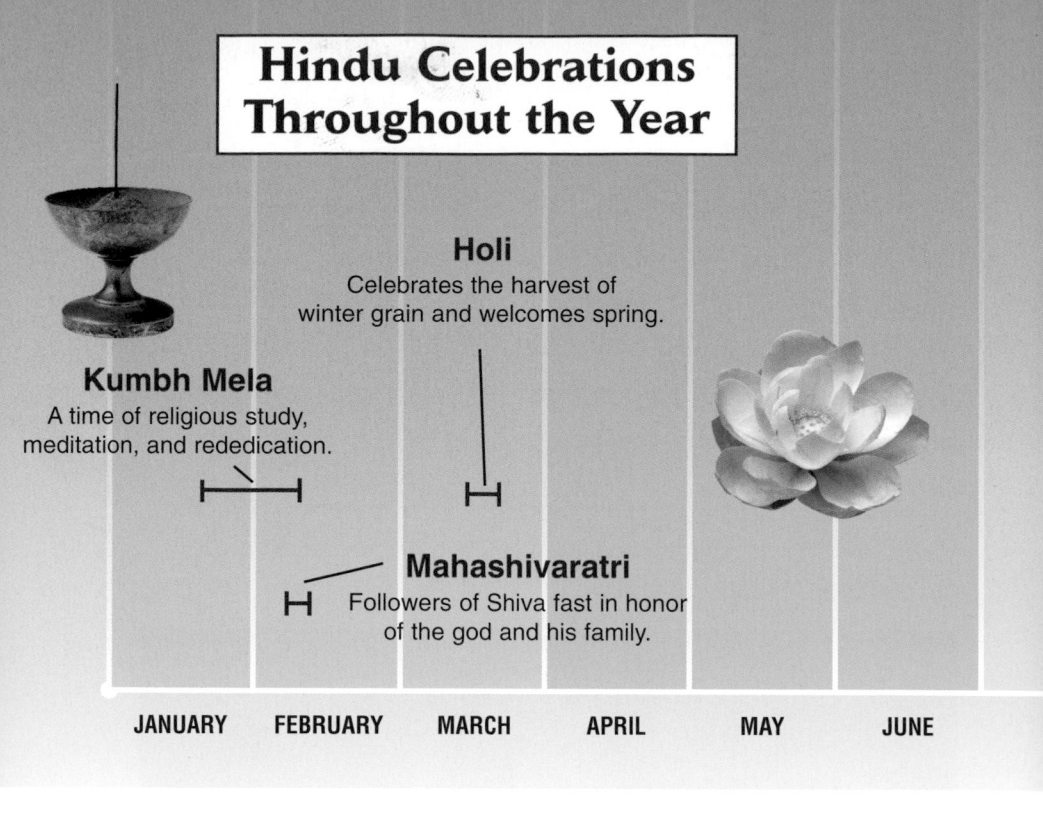

Hindu Celebrations Throughout the Year

Holi
Celebrates the harvest of
winter grain and welcomes spring.

Kumbh Mela
A time of religious study,
meditation, and rededication.

Mahashivaratri
Followers of Shiva fast in honor
of the god and his family.

JANUARY FEBRUARY MARCH APRIL MAY JUNE

shrine. They bathe the image, offer it rice, sandalwood paste, grains, fruits, or flowers, and present it with oil lamps.

On the last day, Ganesha is thanked for his blessings on the house and again carried through the streets. This time, the statue is carried to a river, pond, or beach, and thrown in. The clay image dissolves quickly, ending the annual celebration.

Sometimes entire villages buy huge images of Ganesha, which they put into specially built temples. The image might be traditional, from well-known legends, or fanciful, created from the mind of the artist. Ganesha is always associated with laughter and humor, so his images are sometimes outrageous. He was once portrayed as the lead singer in a band of favorite pop stars, alongside Madonna and Elvis Presley.

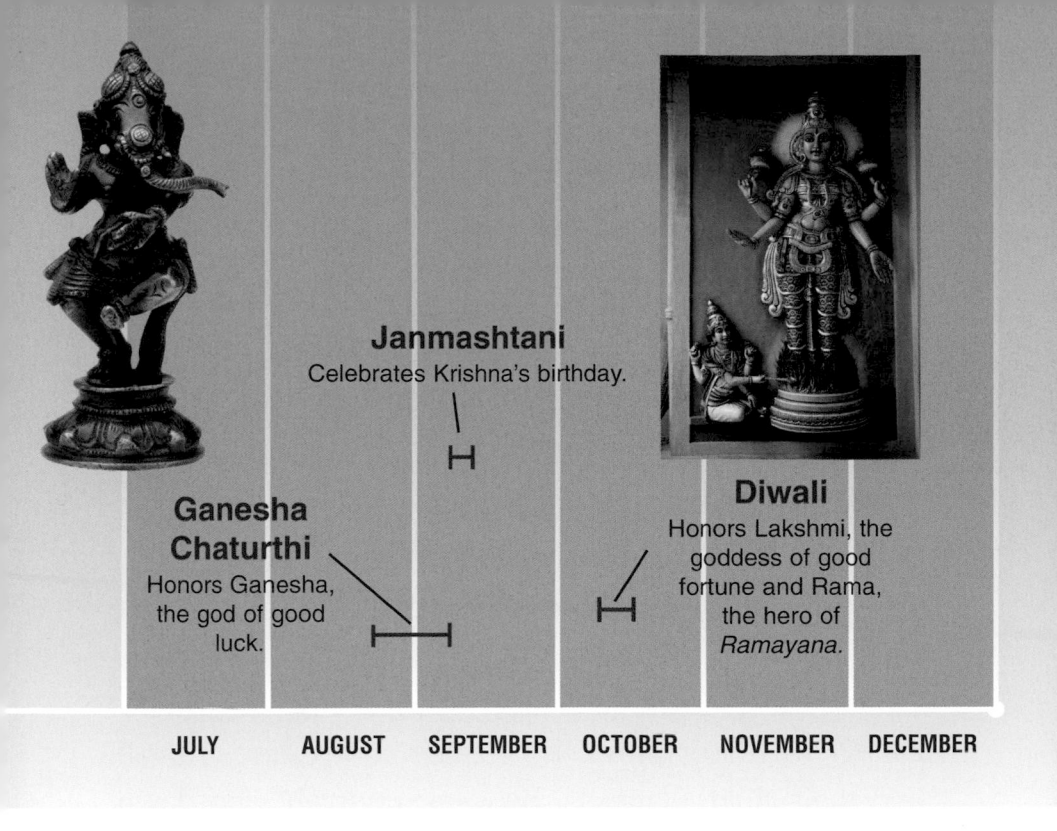

Janmashtani
Celebrates Krishna's birthday.

Ganesha Chaturthi
Honors Ganesha, the god of good luck.

Diwali
Honors Lakshmi, the goddess of good fortune and Rama, the hero of *Ramayana.*

JULY AUGUST SEPTEMBER OCTOBER NOVEMBER DECEMBER

Diwali

One of the most important Hindu festivals is Diwali, celebrated in October. It honors Lakshmi, the goddess of good fortune, and Rama, hero of the *Ramayana.* Diwali is a joyful event, lasting five days. People prepare special foods, watch fireworks, exchange cards and gifts, and light millions of small oil lamps. The lamps are placed by doors and windows and in every shrine and temple. They float along the seashore, on rivers, streams, and ponds.

Bathing Fairs

One of the most serious and contemplative Hindu holidays occurs only once every three years, in January or February. This event, Kumbh Mela, alternates among four holy sites—Allahabad and Haridwar on the Ganges, and Ujjain and Nasik in western India. These colorful events draw millions to bathe in the river, pray, and listen to lectures from gurus, or religious teachers. It is a time for religious study, meditation, and rededication. At the great Kumbh Mela in Allahabad as many as 10 million worshippers camp in tent cities along the Ganges.

Smaller Local Festivals

Many local festivals in India honor a single god or goddess. Some honor the change of seasons or grain harvests. Followers of Shiva in parts of India celebrate Mahashivaratri, the Great Night of Shiva, in February. During the all-night celebration, people fast (go without eating) to honor Shiva, his female companion, Parvati, and their child, Ganesha. Between midnight and dawn, worshippers make offerings of milk, water, grain, and flowers. Followers of Krishna celebrate his birthday, Janmashtani, in early September. An image of baby Krishna is washed with yogurt, ghee (liquid butter), honey, and milk. Afterward, people take turns pushing the image in a swing. Other local festivals include Ratha Yatra, to honor Vishnu, and Sarasvati Puja, in honor of Sarasvati, goddess of wisdom and of the arts. These festivals have changed little in hundreds of years.

The Hindu World Today

Hinduism is as alive and vibrant today as it was three thousand years ago, and its influence can be seen in many cultures. Around the world, people have taken lessons from Hinduism and adapted them to their own lives. Yoga, meditation, vegetarianism, and natural

Although Hindus live in many countries around the world, more than 93 percent live in India.

medicine—all elements of Hinduism—have found their way into Western culture.

Today, India is home to 93 percent of the world's Hindus. However, about 60 million live in other countries. Today Hinduism thrives in Malaysia, Thailand, Bangladesh, Myanmar, and Indonesia. Hindus also live in Africa and the West Indies, Great Britain, the United States, and Canada.

Wherever Hindus have settled, they have taken with them their beliefs, built temples, and worshipped their gods. Young Hindus may grow up citizens of Great Britain, Canada, South Africa, or the United States, but Hindu traditions and culture are still important to them.

FOR FURTHER EXPLORATION

Books

Hitz Demi, *Gandhi*. New York: Simon & Schuster, 2001. Beautiful language and exquisite illustrations tell the life story of Mohandas Gandhi, leader of India's independence from the British Empire.

Anita Ganeri, *Hindu Festivals Through the Year*. North Mankato, MN: Smart Apple Media, 2004. An introduction to the main religious festivals, telling the story behind each and describing how each is celebrated around the world.

Jean "Vishaka" Griesser, *Our Most Dear Friend: An Illustrated Bhagavad-Gita for Children*. Los Angeles: Torchlight, 1996. Presents the essence of the Gita in simple yet captivating text, paintings, and photographs.

Sharukh Husain, *Demons, Gods and Holy Men from Indian Myths and Legends*. New York: McGraw-Hill, 1995. Stories from Hindu mythology and Indian history.

Dilip Kadodwala, *Hinduism*. Chatham, NJ: Raintree/ Steck-Vaughn, 1995. An overview, including the history, scriptures, ceremonies, and customs of Hinduism.

Dianne M. MacMillan, *Diwali: Hindu Festival of Lights*. Berkeley Heights, NJ: Enslow, 1997. The history and traditions of Diwali, and how it is celebrated today.

Kerena Marchant, *Krishna and Hinduism*. North Mankato, MN: Smart Apple Media, 2003. Tells the story of Krishna, one of Vishnu's incarnations, and how his story affects Hinduism.

Victoria Parker, *Ganges*. Chatham, NJ: Raintree/Steck-Vaughn, 2003. An introduction to Hinduism. Includes religious legends, an explanation of shrines and home ceremonies, and holidays and special events.

Ranchor Prime, *Hinduism*. London: Thameside, 2003. An overview of the religion, including gods, beliefs, temples, practices, and holidays.

Angela Wood, *Hindu Mandir*. Danbury, CT: Gareth Stevens/Franklin Watts, 1999. Describes what happens inside a Hindu temple, or *mandir*. Clearly written, with exceptional photographs. Explains the customs and beliefs of Hinduism. Contains a bibliography.

Web sites

Hinduism for School (www.btinternet.com/~vive kananda/schools1.htm). An instructive site sponsored by the Vivekananda Centre of London, with links to such subjects as Hindu symbols, founders, holy men, scriptures, karma, yoga, festivals, and temples. Lots of information.

The Hindu Kids Universe (www.hindukids.org). A multimedia interactive Web site designed to introduce children to Hinduism, its gods, beliefs, stories, and holidays. Beautifully illustrated with lots of brightly colored images.

Holiday Spot (www.theholidayspot.com). A commercial site for the sale of greeting cards and gifts, this site provides information about holidays from various cultures. Includes background information about several Hindu holidays, including Diwali.

Welcome to India (http://home.freeuk.net/elloughton13/india.htm). A multimedia, interactive Web site designed for children seven to nine years old, with cute cartoon characters to lead visitors on a tour of India. Includes a look at the sacred Ganges River and Diwali, the Hindu Festival of Lights. Part of an instructional Web site produced by the Snaith Primary School in East Yorkshire, England.

INDEX

PICTURE CREDITS

ABOUT THE AUTHOR

Charles George taught history and Spanish in Texas public schools for sixteen years. He now lives with his wife of thirty-three years, Linda, in the mountains of New Mexico. Together, they have written more than forty young adult and children's nonfiction books. Charles has written two Lucent books, *Life Under the Jim Crow Laws* and *Civil Rights*. He has also written several KidHaven books—*The Holocaust,* part of the History of the World series; *The Comanche* and *The Sioux,* for The North American Indians series; and *Buddhist* for the What Makes Me A? series. He and Linda also wrote *Texas* for the Seeds of a Nation series.